Practical library of home decoration

The Kitchen

atrium
international

Published by: Atrium International
Ganduxer,115,4ª
08022 Barcelona. Spain
Phone: + 34-93 418 49 10
Fax: + 34-93 211 81 39

email:marketing@atriuminternational.jazztel.es
ISBN: 84-8185-274-0

Printed in Spain

AUTHOR
Francisco Asensio Cerver

PUBLISHING DIRECTOR
Nacho Asensio

TEXTS
Joana Furió

TRANSLATION
Harry Paul

GRAPHIC DESING & LAYOUT
David Maynar
Mar Nieto

Contents

Introduction

Interior design has always designated the kitchen, the room that has to be the life and soul of the house, as the ideal place in which to present new concepts aimed at optimizing organization and comfort.

Prestigious architects employ their creativity and experience to find better ways of planning and distributing kitchens, just as they do for the other rooms often considered more relaxing. Over time, their efforts have reflected changing lifestyles and the kitchen has been granted more space, brighter lighting and more vivid colors as it has taken on new functions.

Today whoever wishes to design a new kitchen, or reform an old one, has to decide what kind of ambience they wish to create. If the person who is going to use the kitchen is not young and therefore not willing to move house every so often, and they want their home to be more than just a collection of furniture and other useful or sentimentally valuable objects from you do not remember where, it is probable that they will have to opt for one of the two contrasting styles which currently dominate the latest trends.

One tendency is the old-fashioned homely look which comes with the hope that its mere appearance will provide solace from the urban stress all around us, transporting us back to a paradise with its smell of freshly baked cakes and home made jam. Back to days gone by when the only technology was manual. The alternative tendency is a pragmatic contemporary style characterized by its unwavering rejection of nostalgia, its defense of clean, crisp lines, pragmatism, and its finishes more akin to a laboratory than to a place for food preparation. Fortunately, between these opposite poles there is a range of models that will enable you to put your personal touch on the final kitchen.

Starting out guided by the basic principles of efficient distribution and ease of use, the design of a modern kitchen must above all meet the particular needs of the user. This means that however captivating a set of furniture or appliances may appear in a catalogue what really counts is that they adapt to the space and budget available. Just like all the other rooms in the house, the kitchen must transmit vitality, making sure that the elements on display give off a welcoming feeling, enticing the family members into cooking and sharing quality time together. The final result will be

determined by the furniture textures, the wall coverings, the flooring, the color combinations, the lighting and the lines of the furniture.

This book is intended to help orientate you through the styles that have been popular over the last few years, revealing the aesthetic and functional details that make working or just being in the kitchen more pleasant. There are no strict rules when it comes to distributing the work areas or how to create a fusion of materials and styles, but avoid getting carried away or being eccentric. Excessive originality, not imagination, is always eventually paid for by more physical effort when decorating, and very possibly it later has to be remodeled, which means more expense. Good space organization first time round pays dividends.

Another key factor is how frequently the kitchen will be used. It is not the same preparing everyday meals as regularly putting on a splendid feast for our friends, winning admiration for our culinary skills. The type of table chosen depends on whether we will take light meals or breakfasts at it or if it will be part of a dining room, either because we have no more room or because we so prefer. Alternatively, we could choose a more professional type of design with special emphasis on the quality of the cooking and preparation utensils if we are highly experienced chefs or enjoy experimenting around the hob. Another possibility is to go for a sparse environment, uncluttered worktops and tables so that the children can play and do their homework while we cook.

The wide palette of materials available for adequately fitting out the kitchen, from the flooring to the ceiling taking in the furniture and accessories, means that it is advisable to consult an expert for the most complicated phases of the reform. It is much simpler to put down a linoleum floor, or paint a wall, than to lay down new floor tiling or to tile a wall up to the ceiling.

This book presents representative models and the most ingenious and versatile solutions for common situations or problems arising from unmovable architectural features (pillars, sloping ceilings or windows in key places). Very often a slight modification in the general design scheme of the furniture (lowering the height, taking advantage of a hollow, removing overhangs) is sufficient to overcome a difficult layout and regain space we had written off as wasted.

As we go through step by step we will see that the golden rule in designing kitchens is common sense: organize the kitchen into clearly established work areas, using the resources we have available to embellish the appearance and detailing. Do not be afraid to get rid of anything that is neither useful nor in anyway makes the space more livable.

Joana Furió

The traditional kitchen used to be defined by its function and normally it was just used for preparing meals which were then taken to the dining room nearby. However, it is becoming more frequent for meals to be eaten in the kitchen, regularly or sporadically, depending on the space available and on if both rooms have been joined together by knocking down the walls.

What ever the case, the work areas are distributed according to the layout of the walls. Basically, there are two types of kitchen unit distributions: built-in or freestanding.

Built in kitchens are the most common in houses built by one constructor or when the furniture is manufactured in lots. The experts recognize their architectural qualities fitting neatly into a room which acts like a mould. In recent years freestanding pieces have made a comeback, endorsed by the desire to break the monotony and to go back to old style country kitchens which were simply put together blending in new furniture and objects as they accumulated over time. This choice is more appropriate if the room has important structural elements (chimneys, windows, recesses, paneled or stone walls, etc) which cannot be hidden away behind furniture.

These variables divide the kitchens up into four basic shapes which refer to the number of walls that come into play: the square, the L shape, the U shape, or, fourthly, just one single front. The disadvantage of being one or more ¡wall short¡ can be made up for by introducing a central island or a peninsula for preparing the food or eating it. The height is all-important if the work is to be carried out comfortably.

Today it is common to combine both formulas, playing with the concepts open and closed, exposed or hidden by the basic pieces of furniture: glass cabinets and dressers can be in front of cupboards and drawers. Moreover, they can include decorative detailing, often made to work in practical ways, that break the monotony of built-in units or continuous block units.

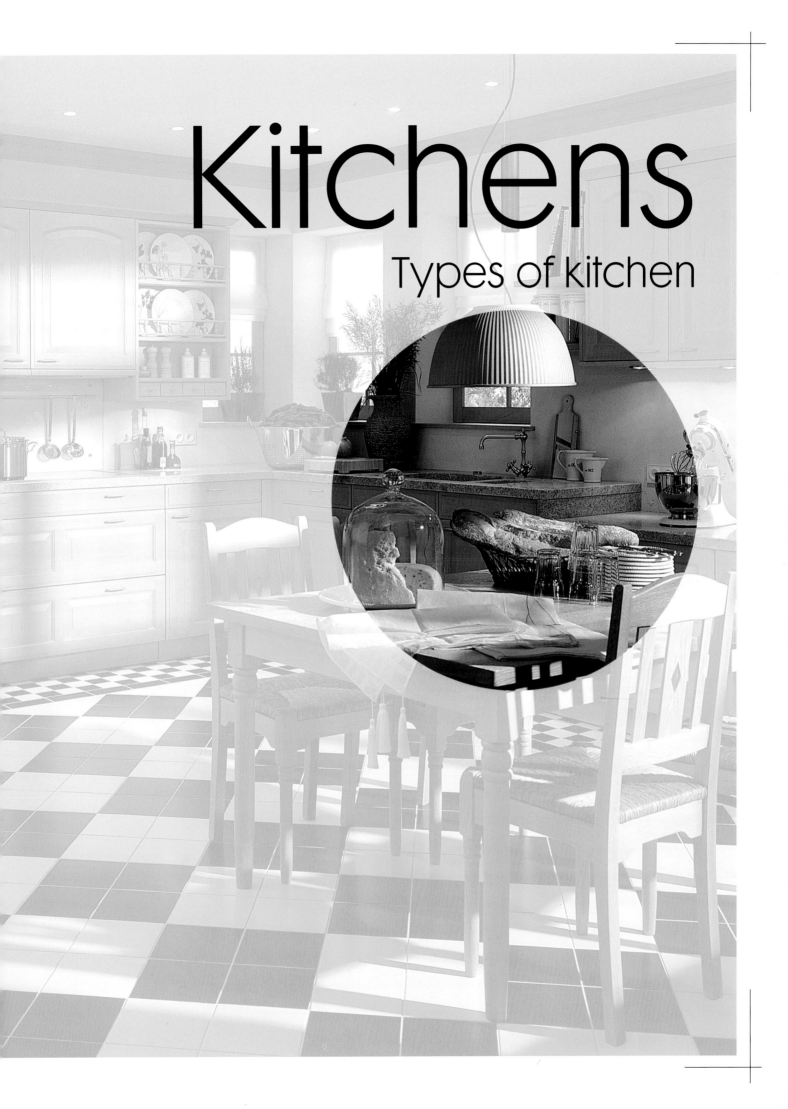

Kitchens

Types of kitchen

A refurbished industrial space

During the nineties pastel colors, like in this upbeat kitchen installed a revitalized industrial space, have caught on, adding one more facet to the wide range of nostalgic throwbacks which appear in home furnishing. Although it is common that styles reminiscent of the past are either country or nineteenth century, there are now so many connotations created by cinema and advertising that even going back a mere thirty years is enough to bring to mind a supposedly more innocent and pleasurable epoch.

In this model the homage to past styles can be seen not only in the yellow pastel color of the lacquered fronts, also reproduced in the set of psychedelic stools, or in the green grooved worktop with its thick maple ledge, but also in the straight lines of all the cupboard and drawer units. Only one edge is rounded.

The brushed stainless steel grips are over a cleft for the finger enabling the doors to be opened easily. Their design is reminiscent of times goneby.

However, modernism comes to the forefront in the design of the cooking and washing equipment, placed in two freestanding units against the wall.

Tips

*This half moon shaped **stylish table** supported on metal legs reinforces the sensation of lightness in the room. Placing it against a pillar is very practical for establishing a division for the living area, evident by the presence of a cupboard by the side of some shelving.*

Intimacy in one environment

When one lives in a little studio like the one in the image, experienced space management is fundamental to avoid a hemmed in, claustrophobic sensation and lack of intimacy.

Here the idea was to create a kitchen in which the three basic functions were all in one run of units - preparation, washing and cooking - and with the inclusion of all luxury gadgets.

The dishwasher is below the sink, fundamental if an neat image is to be projected. There is also a sophisticated Siemens oven, while the fridge and the freezer are hidden away in a radiant cherry colored cupboard to which a table supported by two steel legs has been added for quick, informal meals.

On the wall behind the worktop there is a cylindrical bar for hanging accessories, little pots, kitchen paper. This practical idea livens up the space.

The advantage of the model shown in this photo is that over and above its accessible price, the units are flexible and can be comfortably amplified in a new house with a few modifications, just adding other pieces.

Tips

A small round edged table *is recommendable for a reduced space: its aesthetics are more sympathetic and you are less likely to bump into it. It is supported against one side of the fridge, its height partially concealing the bedroom and giving a greater sensation of space.*

Saving space

When a kitchen barely measures seven square meters and only has two walls against which everything must be fitted, there is no alternative but to limit oneself to what is vital and to rely on the most new-fashioned, versatile ideas.

If the walls are high enough tall cupboards give one or two extra shelving levels or racking. In this kitchen the foldable doors are an aid, both because they weigh less and because they do not bump into other accessories.

Just like in the last model the pivoted panel is a winning formula for saving space. The space at the rear acts as an open cupboard and the front part keeps the most necessary utensils at hand. The fridge and freezer below it have been disguised in a cupboard with an air vent at the top so that they do not have to be separated from the wall.

The oven, hob and smoke extractor with downlighters above the worktop form a compact unit.

In the space behind the door a column of rotating trays ñyou can decide the number- crafted out of different materials, glass, metal and wood, has been installed. The visual lightness means that the reduced dimensions are not depressing.

Once again exemplary organization of the interior equipment is an aid to creating comfortable design.

Tips

Small kitchens *with two walls available can take advantage of height to make up for what they are lacking in width. Modular systems with a good internal space management are best for keeping the work zones uncluttered.*

English style

This spacious kitchen has been designed so that the furniture occupies only two walls and leaves plenty of leeway for the central cooking island.

Without breaking the prevailing traditional style the light ochre milestone worktop and the white fridge provide a contrast to the dark, solid red of the molded wood cupboards opened by the sturdy knobs. Up above there is a run of cabinets with alternating closed doors and glass showcases in which homemade preserves can be seen. The lower units accommodate drawers of different depths and small cupboards with two shelves for the crockery and household items.

However, the most striking part of the kitchen is the cooking zone, totally different in style to the rest of the room, with its gas burners and glass ceramic hob giving away that the owners set very high culinary standards. This is the center of attention both physically; the pure natural light flowing in through the magnificent double pane windows reinforces the visual impact.. The metal, the use of black, the golden edges and the subtly ovaled shape remind us we are in a kitchen of the twenty first century in which nostalgia must be held in check. The secret is in modernism and tradition mutually enhancing each other.

Tips

Metal and wooden racking *systems from which to hang moulds and other utensils have had a second lease of life with new kitchen designs, sometimes replacing the smoke extractor. However, only hang frequently used elements to avoid grease and dust building*

A country style

Today's designs for country style kitchens are a return to traditional values with their feeling of warmth and the pragmatic comfort associated with country and farm houses.

The kitchen is the heart of the house, not only a work place but also where all generations of the family spend time together.

Decorators and experts in interior design affirm that country style kitchens today are based on reminiscences of an ideal past expressed through materials and decorative features. This country vogue is perhaps closest to the kitchens which evoke the Mediterranean or Anglo-Saxon cultures.

The former because of their association with the sun and the art of living in an environment close to nature, stripped bare of superfluous elements. The trait of "English" design is a kitchen of poise and austerity providing a sense of well-being for a closely knit family sheltered from the bleak winter.

In country kitchens care is taken not to hide anything. Instead anything that hints at a pleasurable life, like jars of preserves, porcelain or china crockery, is exhibited.

The independent pantry is as important as the drawers and cabinets fixed to one or more walls. An island for preparing food is also frequent, especially for family kitchens that must have all sorts of gadgets to meet the constant and varied demands of working flat out.

Made to measure country kitchens are not normally built-in, rather they are composed of a series of modular freestanding units in wood.

These projects are artisinal in their design and neither detailing nor fine materials are skimped on because they are kitchens built to last. In an epoch when rushing around is standard, and time is money, adding together ancestral wisdom and cutting edge technology in one space, however simple the finishes may be, gives an air of luxury, dignified tranquility and savoir vivre.

The standard electric appliances are out of sight, hidden away behind the molded wooden cupboard doors, hand painted or varnished.

The smoke extractor is sublimely camouflaged inside the chimney.

The large dimensions of this space mean that various concepts can come into play at the same time. There are high and low cupboards, glass showcases, doors with latticework and shelves that leave their contents visible. The central island worktop is covered in wood matching the other work areas. There are iron bars and hooks for hanging light utensils or recipients. Finally, the dark wood table with its high backed chairs and the antique sideboard with curvaceous columns successfully merge together the upbeat austerity of the modern furniture with the relaxed warmness of the pieces worth saving from the past. The attention to the detailing and the artisanal finishes are a demonstration of the care taken with work in the past.

Combining spaces

In this kitchen the space has been divided up into work areas by a combination of built-in and freestanding furniture.

The metal, wood and glass create a sober yet cheerful classic look, enhanced by the pure finishing lines of the designs.

The two basic concepts in this kitchen are functionality and warmth, with certain colorist reminiscences of the sixties and its open spirit when the strict division of the house according to functions was put in question. Here the kitchen seems designed to be an area for gastronomic experimentation rather than where the family gets together.

The preparation zone is composed of a glass cabinet built in to the wall separating the kitchen from the living room. The internal lighting appears to play with the idea of being able to see within solid objects. Placing a twin bowl sink with one mixer faucet makes the unit perfectly symmetrical.

The laminated amber imitation maple worktop covers all the drawer and cupboard units. They are characterized by their decorated sides and concave edges creating an exemplary finish. Notice the upper drawers and the handles: inside there are flat drawers for storing cutlery and chopping boards.

Tips

The all-purpose oven *is built-in at eye level to a freestanding unit. There are cupboards on either side and below a drawer for utensils and trays. As it is located in front of the cooking zone you do not have to waste energy going back and forth.*

Open on all fronts

This kitchen has a U shaped work space closed off by a built-in cupboard between two columns. In the middle of the cupboard there is an oven and microwave at eye level. The dark glass door and rim breaks the monotony of the white laminated wood fronts which go down to the metal plinth all round the room.

The preparation zone is divided into two sections. The upper part is occupied by three cupboards with a crystal door displaying the contents. Inside there are four transparent shelves which complement the sense of lightness. The vertical stainless steel handles run up almost all the length of the doors, like on the other drawers and cupboards. Built-in pin lights under the cupboards illuminate the white laminate wooden edged worktop. Another original detail is the steel bar along the far wall for hanging small utensils and accessories. The sink section is divided into three: the drainer, the main bowl and a smaller one for soaking.

The third side of the U shape is a work area which is also for serving the small meals on the eating counter. It is finished in dark wood.

The main feature is its height, planned so that the person cooking can communicate with the eaters or other users.

Tips

The small hob *for preheating food or keeping it warm while the other dishes are prepared is in fact the reinvention of a hollow space existent in the old coal ovens. It is a handy idea when working hectically in the kitchen or when people are always dropping in to eat.*

A key role for aluminum

What first catches the eye here is the way the two basic materials of contemporary minimalist tendency kitchen design, crystal and metal, bring out the best in each other. Wood plays a subtle role as a complementary element for the worktops and for the handles of the shelves, containers, rollers and for the herb pots.

Aluminum is the principal structural element in all the furniture.

The intention was to design a kitchen of the future, not with an image of sociality but rather as a precise laboratory dedicated to looking after our health through gastronomic art. With this objective in mind, the firm's top designer concentrated on durability, hygiene and precision in the work. Another consideration was the search for ecological, recyclable materials and formulas. All paints and toxic products were ruled out in the trimmings and

finishes. This roomy kitchen has been divided into three work areas.

The storage function is taken care of by a series of low wide cupboards. The single bowl sink is in the middle of the unit with a stainless steel mixer faucet.

The upper cupboards are large laminated tempered glass sliding cabinets. Inside there are two shelves. The worktop is illuminated by built-in pin lights

Tips

The front of curvaceous sheets *joins flawlessly with the handle. Both are made of aluminum because it allows highly elaborate detailing, is resistant to water, solid and flexible.*

A very small space

This tiny kitchen -there is little over a meter between the facing cupboard fronts- almost makes it seem as if we were on a recreational boat due to its concise design. However, it is in fact part of a revamped flat in which the owners have refused to renounce any of the basic elements necessary for the kitchen to be a comfortable place, all the space fully taken advantage of. The design is in the form of a U with radiant varnished chestnut wood cupboards and drawers all around on the lower level creating a natural feel. The metal grips add the contrast. The only cabinet fixed to the wall is for draining crockery.

The crystal door opens upwards and, to the right, there are four squarish filing drawers. All the worktop and the wall panel in the preparation zone is aluminum. Above the worktop, below the cabinet, there is a bar for hanging utensils, pans and sieves. The glass ceramic cooking hob is fitted into a recess together with the smoke extractor. Placing tiles around the upper part of the hood is an efficient way of reducing the cleaning work.

Below the large window which makes the whole space seem much more roomy there is a two bowl stainless steel sink unit. The dishwasher is hidden away in a gap at one end of the worktop. The two ovens have been placed at eye level in the unit on the left.

Tips

A small space must *be efficiently managed so that it is not cluttered. What does not fit widthwise must go heightwise, skillfully fitting in open and closed furniture and filling the gaps which are normally left empty.*

Sophistication from simplicity

In this kitchen simplicity is turned into sophistication by laying out the unit absolutely symmetrically and by employing basalt gray, slightly evocative of a professional space. The structure of this compact block, including the hod and the one bowl sink, is completed at either end by two identical column cupboards.

Although the main storage function is assigned to the lower cupboards, the two long thin ones at the top, which open upwards, can hold plates and glasses.

Being higher than the center of the block they also avoid everything being straight lined. In their base downlighters for the worktop have been fixed, complementing the light provided by the Siemens smoke extractor. In the wall zone in the middle of the cupboards there are small shelves and bars for han-

ging utensils, gadgets, and kitchen paper etc. A lectern gives a less austere image.

The crystal doored cupboard with metal edges and handles and internal lighting marks where the kitchen turns into the living area, maintaining the touch of sophistication and the high score for functionality.

Tips

One wall *is sufficient for a kitchen if the work areas are arranged rationally. This formula is the most apt for people who seldom eat or cook at home.*

The washing zone

The place where the sink is installed is an essential element of any kitchen and careful attention must be paid to ensure an effective and ergonomic solution. It is necessary to measure the distance from the hob and the worktop and the depth of the bowls. Finally, it must be decided whether the draining board is above the sink or a continuation of the worktop.

The choice of materials is important. Wood and synthetic materials like Corian, silestone, asterite and many others available in the market, have the advantage of being less likely to break the glassware. Granite dries more rapidly but things shatter or crack easily when dropped on it.

Whether it is against the wall or located on an island, the sink always needs splashbacks to avoid staining.

Cleaning away waste

As modern living produces so many waste materials, it is wise to tackle their elimination rationally so as to avoid smells and untidiness. It is common to place the organic residues and non-recyclable materials in the standard garbage bag. Paper, glass, tins and plastic packets can be sorted and taken to their respective deposits provided by the state authorities.

Kitchen furniture designers have come up with all sorts of ideas for disposing of waste. There are bins divided internally or stackable units for non-rotting waste which do not have to be hidden away in the traditional place below the sink.

Lately the shredder garbage disposal has come into fashion. Installed in the sink bowl, or in a whole cut in the worktop surface, there is a direct chute to the waste bin so that peelings and other residues fall directly into the garbage without staining the floor.

More sophisticated, but gradually becoming a must-have in big families or professional kitchens, is the electric can crusher which means greater volumes of garbage can be conveniently stored before being thrown out.

Two bowls with a draining board for the crockery, an example of the plasticity of materials today.

An example of a kitchen island: it is a great idea for organizing the space.

A touch of sobriety

The generous space available means it is possible to create a dining room with visual contact with the kitchen work area.

The lower cupboards and drawer units have left the walls bare.

The white fronts in the kitchen area and the beige in the dining room remind one of an office, an idea continued with the round table on a central steel support, the wooden backed stackable chairs and the dark varnished parquet floor.

The one piece light colored synthetic worktop, with a sink countersunk into it, stands out.

Thanks to the light coming in through the enormous window and bounced off the white walls, the formal austerity of this kitchen, inspired by a not too over-the-top seventies style, is neither oppressive nor lacking in imagination, rather it blends together practicality and neatness.

The work area has been installed along the only total free wall, grouping together the utensils for cooking, washing and food preparation. All the units are the same width; the fronts are laminated and lacquered in dark green.

Only the control panel along the top gives away that there is a dishwasher. The granite worktop and splashback along all of the back wall match the tiled flooring, reflecting the natural light. The modern mixer faucet and one bowl sink are of stainless steel.

In fact, metal materials are used not only in the work zone but also for the dining room table, the three small halogen lamps that hang just above it, and the chair frames, although the seats and backrests are plastic.

Tips

The small television *perched high up on a bracket is a practical solution for it does not get in the way, is visible from all angles and there are no reflections. Put a power point as close as possible to avoid dangling, unsightly cables.*

A summer kitchen

When one has an apartment by the beach it is normally used for relaxed cooking, not so demanding as on labor days. Therefore it is not necessary to have all the sophisticated gadgets, just the sufficient. The kitchen in the photo has been organized along one wall. Lack of space has ruled out any upper wall cupboards.

The only space accessible was in the corner where the stainless steel smoke extractor is. In the little gap there is a wooden shelf on which pots are placed.

Along all the width of the smoke extractor there is a stainless steel bar for hanging utensils. This practical, in-fashion option leaves the utensils at hand right above the glass ceramic hob. The worktop is of wood stripes with a natural tone, multi-layered edge.

The cupboard and drawer fronts all have long handles and are either of varnished wood or a blue veneer, except the two crystal fronted drawers for casserole dishes, situated below the hob.

The innovative sink built into the worktop has two coverable containers which are directly linked to the waste disposal avoiding the possibility of dirtying the floor

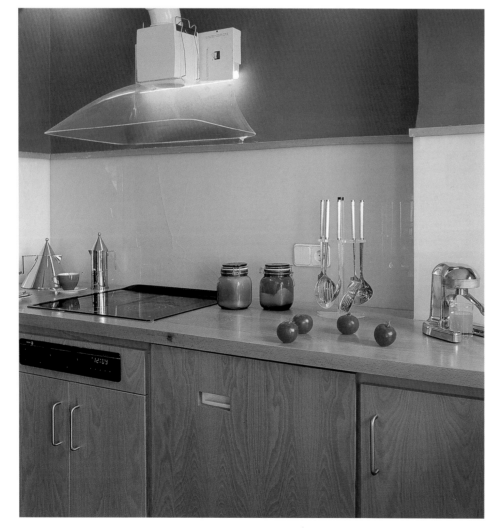

Tips

Heavily used kitchens *greatly benefit from the details that improve their daily functioning, like this imaginative sink with two holes for disposing of the peels directly into the waste bucket. Behind the mixer faucet there is a strip for placing the cleaning utensils.*

Parallel lines

A long, narrow kitchen has to use all the height of the wall and rely on built-in equipment and the sense of order created by crisp lined furniture. The kitchen in the photo is organized into two spaces demarcated by the columns just after the oven and microwave. The interior part accommodates the hob and sink zones, facing each other. The fronts are of white natural wood laminates, except the cooking worktop which is in aluminum.

Only on one side are there high cupboards; on the other side is the smoke extractor.

The washing zone consists of two different sized stainless steel bowls countersunk into the white synthetic worktop with a multi-layered wooden rim. The middle part of the wall is paneled to make it resistant and easy to clean. This pragmatic approach to storage resorts to internally divided units that keep the most used items at hand. In the far section is the dishwasher and opposite it a three door built-in cupboard for provisions and cleaning materials. Although the light from the window reaches all the room and takes away any sensation of narrowness during the day, spotlights have been fixed in the ceiling and there is a light strip underneath the cupboards for task lighting.

Tips

It is becoming more common **to use two energy sources,** *gas and electricity, for cooking. This glass ceramic hob has two gas burners for big and small pots. There is little chance of running out of energy to cook with.*

A clear view and inspiration

In this kitchen special attention has been paid to the communication between the two spaces and the harmony of the furniture so that the daily activities can be carried out effortlessly without anything getting in the way. This type of kitchen invites all the family, and even guests, to lend a hand.

Two elements are the focal point in this design aimed at imitating the warmth of the traditional family kit-chen combined with the technolo-gical and ergonomical perfection of contemporary styles.

One striking effect is the curva-ceous worktop which aids the amplification of the space behind the glass ceramic hob without clut-tering the sides, normally taken over by plates, pans and ingredients. The second striking feature is the modern sink island, marked off by two columns offering great practi-

cal and decorative possibilities. There is also a counter for eating slightly above the worktop.

It was also possible to include a column of swivel mesh trays, bars for hanging items and other accessories to keep the fresh produce and breakfast utensils visible and at hand.

Tips

A small gap between low cupboards can be put to good use for a double level bottle cabinet which slides outwards. The shelves and racking are designed to support the weight without any spillage. However, it is not suitable for wines because they should be stored horizontally.

Eating in the kitchen

In this spacious kitchen and family dining area the honor of occupying the center of the room has been given over to the original glass topped table illuminated by a fanciful chandelier. Its futuristic image, an amalgam of metal and crystal, contrasts with the other kitchen furniture with its synthetic white fronts, wood sides and cream gray worktops.

While in the washing area all the cupboards are on an aluminum baseboard, the units destined to cooking and storage, and the double oven piece, are elevated off the floor to make cleaning simpler.

The units have been deliberately placed at different heights and some elements, the plates, cutlery and glassware, have been left visible and neatly ordered on shelves fixed to the cooker specially fitted out for this purpose. The lower height of the far cupboard has enabled a wine rack to be placed on top of it.

The wall of the cooking zone has been paneled in wood to make it more resistant to the ravages of food preparation. The three drawers below are as wide as the worktop and deeper than those of the adjacent unit. An unused gap has been left in the middle of the two blocks.

Tips

*The majority of **smoke extractors** cover all of the cooking area and allow the external surface area to be used for storing bottles, jars, spices and herbs, thus leaving the worktops free for products and recipients in use.*

The food preparation zone should be a resistant, wide surface so that all the products and recipients can be used comfortably. In addition, it is recommendable it is conveniently located, preferably next to the sink and the hob, with all the gadgets at

The most common materials are stainless steel, granite, wood, formica, Corian or other synthetic materials which lately have become highly regarded in the market. All of them must be anti-flammable, resistant, clean, easy to install and to keep looking

hand, so as not to waste time in wearisome journeys. Finally, good lighting is important because tired eyes make the work harder going.

The worktops are the fundamental part of this zone and must therefore be given a touch of color to harmonize or contrast with the other furniture. Resistance, durability and cleanliness are ensured by choosing the right materials which can stand up to intensive use. The finishes must be safe and practical both on the flat surface and on the seams next to the sink or the hob.

good, visually impacting and offer good value for money.

Choosing the material not only depends on our budget or aesthetic considerations but also on making the worktop compatible with the rest of the furniture. Wood has a homely feeling and evokes an artisinal period, while aluminum looks professional and is resistant to whatever it may be put through, as if it were built for life. The experts recommend steering clear of plastic because it mixes badly with food.

This kitchen is completed by the cupboard supported on very striking metal istiltsi, matching the rest of the room. Its height and capacity make it suitable for a larder or crockery cabinet, depending on whether it is placed in the kitchen or dining room. It is divided into two identical compartments with different colored fronts to break the monotony and to tie it in with the rest of the work zone.

In this L shaped kitchen the combination of glass fronted and closed units gives it a fresh, modern feel.

This kitchen is strictly divided into three areas.

The preparation zone is against the wall and consists of a run of waist high units which include drawers for pans and a cupboard for the waste disposal.

The dishwasher is underneath the smooth worktop enhanced by the edge of unlaminated natural wood. The white sink area includes a wide bowl, a draining board and a sliding chopping board. Up above there are two layers of glass fronted cupboards.

The cooking zone is marked off by a freestanding unit on the other side of which is the dining area. The dining table is wood topped and has a metal frame, remindful of school desks in the seventies.

A peninsula in the middle

This kitchen is L shaped thanks to the peninsula coming out of one wall and bending round to offer space for cooking and an informal eating area.

The side dedicated to food preparation is made up of laminated aluminum units and wide horizontal handles along all the width of the drawers. There are only cupboards, also in aluminum, below the sink. Their grips are vertical.

The aluminum worktops are soft on the eye and easy to clean.

Above the sink and worktop there are two levels of glass fronted cabinets, more like a bookcase in a living room than the typical kitchen.

The fact that they are fixed to the wall in the rear part, and not supported by brackets, reinforces the sensation of lightness for it is as if they were suspended in the air.

The modules have been divided symmetrically. In the middle are the objects used less often.

The space between the two hanging cupboards is sufficiently wide to use it as a dresser or kitchen bookshelf.

Tips

The glass ceramic *hob directly integrated into the aluminum worktop is easier to clean. The seams between the two surfaces must be flawlessly sealed so that dirt does not become ingrained. With today's technical progress improved cleaning and preservation materials are available which will keep the hob looking new for years.*

Wood as the leit motiv

This kitchen, designed for a city-living family, exploits the beauty of oak and its radiant, cozy good looks which contrast with the metal handles, the smoke extractor and the stainless steel edged worktop.

The work zone incorporates the oven, built into a cupboard composed of three modules, the hob and the sink.

The height of the cupboard leaves room on top for accessories used daily and for a wood shelf for the cookery books.

The three sections of the cupboard, to which there has not been assigned a specific function, are closed of by a roller blind now quite in fashion for storing electrical appliances. The four burner glass ceramic hob is built into the cooking zone. Notice the clever way the knives are stored ruling out the possibility of inadvertently cutting yourself.

The aluminum smoke extractor is camouflaged by the wall color, although its rim with tiny decorative orifices make it stand out a little.

On the upper right side there is a small glass, rectangular cabinet which opens upwards. On the base there is a series of spotlights to provide task lighting for the worktop.

Tips

A sheet of glass, *supported on aluminum pillars, which acts a food counter, funky high aluminum chairs with thin legs and an architectural lamp all work together to make the island unobtrusive. Its open sides enable all the family breakfast items to be stored together.*

Aesthetics and functionality

This kitchen forms part of one room in which the lounge and the dining area are also situated. The kitchen space is marked out by the white, easy to clean tiles. What first catches our eye is the multi-colored front of the half-moon shaped island between the cooking and service areas. However, a more careful look will reveal the good taste and fine sense of balance between aesthetics and functionality. At both ends of the island, housing a glass ceramic hob with four burners and an all aluminum periscopic smoke extractor coming down from the ceiling, there are two floor to ceiling columns which apart from providing support have other practical purposes.

On the columns, besides the two pairs of downlighters fixed higher up, there are a series of circular ledges, some of them swiveling, for assorted uses. On the left there is a

circular wood table, supported on an arm, for serving breakfast or quick meals for one or two people eating together.

The front of this built-in kitchen unit combines classic features, like the white module cupboards and drawers with simple wide handles, with other rather more daring features, among which the choice of materials like the aluminum mesh to cover the door space and the unusual pentagon shape of the upper cupboards catch the eye.

Tips

Some prismatic shades screwed to the wall tiles, matching them for originality, and to the cupboard bottoms, provide specific lighting. The rest of the room takes advantage of the light sources spread around the room.

Lighting

As far as is possible the kitchen should enjoy good natural lighting because not only does it make the room seem bigger (above all if bounced off light colored furniture and walls) but

plus necessary for appliances must not be occupied by lamps in continuous use. Today the most frequent type of lighting are spotlights built into the ceiling. Although they are low voltage

also it livens up the space and makes the daily routine of preparing and cooking the food more enjoyable. In addition to natural light it is necessary to have at least one specific source of artificial light for the cooking and preparation zone. In fact, the ideal set up is to have as many light sources as there are independent zones in the kitchen. Lighting can be fitted inside the cupboards or larders.

One of the reasons why it is easy to illuminate a kitchen is that all types of lighting are admissible: bulbs, fluorescent tubes, halogens, or even candles for an intimate meal. To improve efficiency and safety loose hanging cables must be avoided a

they offer intense light and do not dazzle. Fluorescent tubes under the cupboards provide specific lighting for worktops and are not expensive, though eventually they may start to "hum". An alternative to these two possibilities is to install a rail of spotlights. They are cheap and easy to set up but they accumulate dust and give off heat.

For a one off use, or in an unimportant corner, a temporary lamp can be clipped on. The advantage is that the light can be very concentrated but take care the cable is safely positioned. Finally, lights fitted into niches or recesses in the wall are a good solution for high ceilings.

In this kitchen-studio everything has to be protected from the humidity, dust and dirt. The piece in which the oven is installed, designed to be easily cleaned, can be used for keeping kitchen utensils or work items. In the same way, the island is available for kitchen purposes or for doing office work.

The secret lies in being systematic, organizing the space intelligently and not permitting any superfluous elements.

This is another example of how using resistant and all-purpose surfaces, like crystal, stainless steel and lacquers, and adding in more daring tones, in this case cobalt blue, emerald green and burgundy red, enables the decorator to improve on the traditional image of the cooking space and its typical connotations (hustle and bustle, producing waste materials and general messiness) and transform it into a strictly functional area in which high tech has eliminated the mentioned drawbacks as much as possible. The kitchen unit then becomes a professional work space with the central island and the crystal dining table, once it is cleared of the plates and appliances used for enjoying food, is a convenient work desk, turning the zone into an extension of the office.

A kitchen with a view

A completely glass wall with a door leading into the garden has not been an obstacle for the distribution of the work areas in this kitchen designed to prepare meals for a small hotel or an exclusive vacation resort.

The light that filters through the windows, all of them frosted except in the corner, is more than sufficient to intensify the natural luminosity of the walls painted pale green and the wood cupboard fronts matching the food preparation table in the middle.

The biggest wall is used as a storage and preparation area with an L shaped worktop cut out of one single piece of granite. The sink is built-in (observe the adjacent hole for throwing away the waste) and behind it there is a granite splashback with a metal bar. The shelf in the crystal cabinet on the right is also of granite. The amount of space available on the walls, organized into cupboards and drawers below and little units with shelves above, lightens the sensation of heaviness normally transmitted by wood finishes.

Tips

The wide horizontal hob *has above it a smoke extractor which comes down out of the ceiling ñit was not possible to attach it to the wall. The lack of decorative details completes the kitchen design and reinforces the mood. The steel handles along nearly all the width of the drawers and cupboards accentuate the austere professional discipline.*

Three basic activities are realized in the kitchen: food preparation, cooking and washing and each one of them must have its own space without anything getting in the way. Depending on the size of the room and family habits other activities can also be included, like dining and laundry, with the corresponding areas clearly defined and demarcated.

In theory the separation between the areas should be based on how one normally goes from one area to another, establishing a sequence which aids the work flow. The design experts have established the ideal triangle for an L shaped kitchen in which every area is at an equal distance from the others. However, whatever the kitchen is like, an effort will be made to organize the areas to help the cooking process, from the preparation through to washing the dishes in the sink or dishwasher at the end. Items can be stored all round the walls but try to keep food a little distance away from the preparation zone.

In a medium sized or big kitchen, the separation of the areas is marked out by furniture, columns or a skilled combination of materials when used as something more than decorative elements. An example of this would be to separate the dining area from the preparation zone by a pillar or an island. Distinct colors and furniture that does not completely block the view also mark off zones. Another option is to define the areas with the flooring, placing a material specially appropriate for the kitchen in this space and leaving the rest of the home unchanged when you are dealing with a studio or gallery kitchen.

The space can be identified as a kitchen by having visible references (showcases, crystal doors, panels, etc) or alternatively the activities can be hidden away. However, always bear in mind the relationship with the other rooms in the house so that the style is coherent.

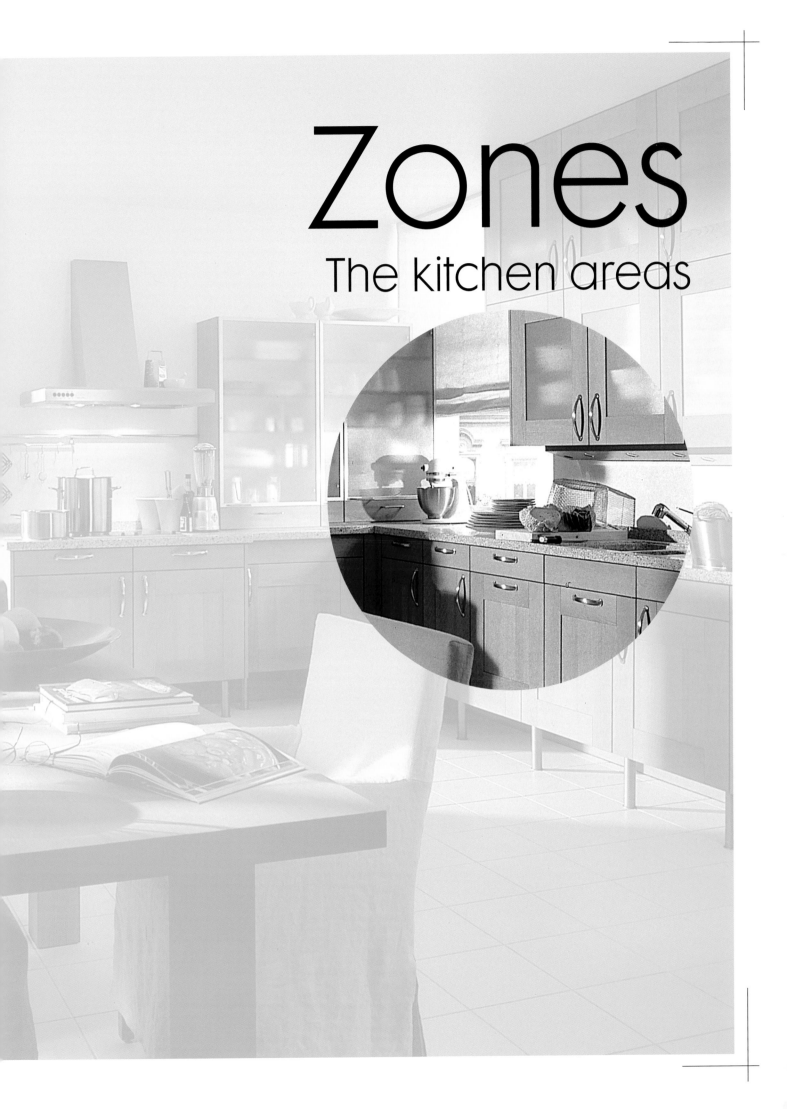

Zones

The kitchen areas

A vanguardist atmosphere

In this kitchen the furniture has been set against two walls which come together in a column and not in an awkward corner. The upper cupboards in the washing and preparation zone, lacquered in granite, do not go as far as the ceiling so as to allow the light through from the windows behind.

The drawers in the lower units have various types of separators and can withstand weights up to sixty kilograms. The gap on the wall in between has been covered with glass showcasing and power sockets have been installed. In the stainless steel sink zone there are paneled splashbacks. Below is the dishwasher and the garbage disposal. The two white doors create a tonal counterfoil which is repeated in the area next to the oven door, located between two modular units. The cooking and preparation zone occupies a spacious central zone suffi-

cient to prepare the food on the gas and electric burners. Beneath the imitation cristalan granite worktop there are different shaped drawers. The flatter ones are for cutlery and kitchen knives, and the deeper ones for pots, trays and pans, or for the tablecloths and serviettes used daily. The gray cupboard on the right is deep enough to store the everyday crockery. Its imitation aluminum roller blind door is ideal for avoiding bruises on the legs as kitchens can become quite busy at peak moments.

Tips

The upper cupboard *units can be opened upwards or can be left ajar thanks to the double hinge set. In general, it is recommendable to use the upper cupboards for storing the crockery and glassware, while the lower units are suitable for the heavy recipients.*

Cooking for big groups

This model was conceived as a space intended for the preparation of square meals on a large scale and therefore the kitchen has been set up as an island, both sides of which can be worked at.

Due to the demands placed on this professional kitchen two types of cookers had to be installed: gas and electric. And to take away the correspondingly high amounts of smoke and fumes given off, two industrial stainless steel smoke extractors coming down from the ceiling were fitted.

The black marble worktops are on the same level as the burners, while the ends of the island are of thick, radiant pinewood, rounded at the edges to make an otherwise too compact piece more harmonious and manageable. The lower part has been divided up into white lacquered modular units with a cupboard at each end inside of which there are three shelves for the crockery.

In the middle of the island there are four wide drawers, the bottom ones having a decorative black triangle and very wide steel handles to emphasize the way they daringly turn their back on standard family kitchens.

The wall has been used principally as a storage area in which high and low cupboards of different capacities have been installed.

Tips

A clever idea *was to place the two high ovens at eye level on the extreme right where they do not get in the way at all. Their doors fit in with the black rectangles painted on some fronts in the kitchen and give more unity to the whole working area.*

Luxurious organization

The image of everything in this kitchen is so restrained it is almost austere, like a monastery.

The panels on the wall and on the interiors and faces of the upper cupboards are of dark wood, the same as the bases and on top of the oven fitted between two cupboards. Only some discrete opaque crystal doors which open upwards allow through the fluorescent light from inside the cupboards .

Metal is also used for the large, modern stainless steel sink and for the decorative cooking hood, to which no detail that goes beyond its strict functional necessities has been added.

The worktop with built-in hob and interspersed marble turns sobriety into elegance. The cupboard units, deeper in the cooking zone to enable comfortable work, mark off the different zones and

understatement is again manifest in the aluminum rectangular unadorned smoke extractor.

The laminated white faces of the lower cupboards and drawers and of the built-in dishwasher with simple gray handles add luminosity and style, a style which puts pragmatism first and shies away from striking visual impacts.

Tips

*Sometimes it is necessary to install units of **different heights** and widths to make the work easier. The cooking zone is lower to avoid straining the eyes or back when working with the food or keeping an eye on the stews.*

The experts recommend that the cooking zone is located near a sink, facing a wall, and is next to a space in which the saucepans can be placed before they go on the burners. A lot of effort is saved if easy to clean materials, like stainless steel or vitreous enamel, are used. Large controllable knobs also help the chef. The energy source can be either gas -its flame is more easily regulated- or electricity.

In the last decade the kitchen hob has benefited from a genuine revolution. There are various possibilities ranging from the simpler gas burner through to the convection oven, considered the cooker of the future. Gas hobs offer the most controllable form of cooking.

The glass ceramic hobs are circular and rapidly start a homogeneous cooking process exploiting the fact that the heat penetrates more easily. The halogen burners instantly heat the surface and spread the heat uniformly. The induction plates do not have a heat or flame center because the electromagnetic field only heats the recipient. As the plate remains cool it avoids accidents and does not burn any spilled food.

If you cannot make up your mind, get the best of both worlds with a model which has both energy sources. Alternatively two different hobs can be installed.

There is a series of accessory elements which are gradually finding a place in ahead of the game kitchens, like wok rings, griddles, ultra-rapid central burners, flame failure device shut offs and simmer settings and which indicate the high technological, health and safety demands being placed on the kitchen design industry.

Smoke extractors can be decorative, independent, telescopic, hidden away inside a piece of furniture or columnless. All of them have their own lighting. It is recommendable that the extraction power be controllable. Choose a quiet one: humming becomes irritating.

For an L shaped kitchen an island is a practical idea.

Good design does not leave out the latest technological advances which keep a room with few windows free of bad smells.

The external appearance of this kitchen, its size and ostentatious lines, sets out to be a subtle homage to the nineteen fifties. The combination of laminates and thick chrome edges inevitably reminds us of the films from this epoch. Who doesn't remember the impressive cars James Dean and Elvis used to drive? The symmetrical organization of the units is a sound idea because it enables other modules to be added on according to the space available and the budget. The steel and white porcelain handles and the black granite worktop are practical for their long-lasting qualities. The cooking zone has been divided into two: the glass ceramic hob on the cooking island and the eye level oven in the column cupboard.

An outstanding kitchen

The lay out of the kitchen, in a U shape to take advantage of all the walls, and the soft pastel yellow tones create a sensation of calm enhanced by the intense orange tone of the lateral columns and the upper front part of the wall where the washing zone is located.

The cooking space is on a small peninsula that comes out of the wall and is topped by a thick granite worksurface matching the other worktops, which, however, are synthetic. The curvaceous edge of the double low cupboard stands out. Its top is used as a work counter and the elegance of its finish breaks the predictability of straight lines.

The oven is built into a three piece modular unit seen on the right. It has only two levels, and just like the four door gray cupboard its top acts as a shelf. All the units are

dedicated to storage and the fridge and dishwasher are placed as frees-tanding units.

The steel and glass smoke extractor is combined with the decorative but very practical adja-cent shelves.

Tips

The side which supports this **little worktop** is wide enough for a low cupbo-ard to fit in. Inside it is divided into three shelves suitable for supporting all types of products and objects, even long life food products which benefit from being stored away from other items.

An all-purpose table

The current proliferation in the big European cities and out of town shopping malls of shops specializing in good looking competitively priced furniture has meant a revolution in kitchen design as the ìdo it yourselfì message has been consolidated, despite the traditional conservatism of the kitchen and its modular units.

The unvarnished pinewood work bench would look just at home in the inside of a garage as in this country inspired kitchen.

The table's first function is to provide a work area for food preparation, and, secondly, to store objects which have no natural storing space.

The two pairs of hooks at both ends are other signs of functionality. It is noticeable the little importance given to style, the attitude manifested by the arrangement bestows character on the rest of the environment.

Everything, from the wooden shelves on the wall to the hangers for sieves and utensils, is practical.

In line with the ìtwo by twoî philosophy, a pair of spotlights provide specific lighting.

Tips

The table top must *jut out considerable to avoid getting snagged on the hooks underneath. Although unvarnished wood keeps well, it must be well sandpapered so you do not get splinters, neither in your hands nor in the food. This is very important for hygiene.*

Storage

Big containers

Over the years it has become more frequent to replace the traditional pantry with a large larder cupboard manufactured according to the most advanced criteria of internal space organization.

Now from their design desk the creator guarantees the functionality having considered the optimum distribution of the internal shelving, the depth and the separations so that the products stored are neatly visible, accessible and ventilated. Steel shelves have the advantage of allowing the air to circulate and are easy to clean.

Wood never goes out of fashion: its strong points are that it bears the weight well and adds a country touch. Granite is good for the central shelf and for storing fresh products at room temperature (cheeses, fruit, etc.).

The inside drawers are for bigger products or for keeping fresh vegetables and bread out of the light. The doors can slide open, or be foldable, and as long as they do not block up the room too much, they can swing open in the standard way.

Small containers

Besides the standard low cupboard units, small drawers or containers are manufactured in materials which complement wood (wicker, mesh, metal and plastic) specifically for storing provisions at room temperature. Eggs, certain cheeses and fruit can all be kept in this way. Some furniture stores, or accessory stores, still sell containers for keeping the food fresh.

Cold storage:Fridges

Fridges can be installed as freestanding units or camouflaged inside a cupboard. The former can be moved around; sometimes they even have their own wheels. Camouflaged fridges are built-in and match the rest of the furniture. In both cases ensure the air can circulate.

A rustic kitchen for a country house.

In this kitchen the designers have tried to recreate the atmosphere of the country houses which were typified by the freestanding pieces accumulated over the years baring witness to the progress made and the improved standard of living.

Nevertheless, the basic furniture is composed of high and low cupboard units intermixed with shelves and white wall spaces so as not to clutter up the room too much.

The work space forms an L shape leaving an area in the center to install a dining table against one of the unoccupied walls. A pair of blue painted benches provide a color counterfoil for the monotony of the wood prevailing all around the kitchen, even in the flooring which is wood planks a little darker than the other elements.

The simple wood moldings on the large doors are reminiscent of artisanal carpentry from other epochs. The unpretentious decoration on the metal handles add class: rustic does not mean coarse or basic. Over the solid white sink unit -note the space to leave scrubbing utensils- an open shelf unit enables small items, like the coffee or tea set, to be left at hand. The cornice in the upper part embellishes the cupboard, hinting at the durableness of this unostentatious design.

The cooking hob is located on the longest wall but there is no oven underneath, leaving the

space free for a metal mesh on which to place the saucepans. That this is a room where there is daily hustle and bustle can be seen from the utilitarian black granite worktop, the splashback and the traditional chimney inside of which the smoke extractor is disguised. Cans and tins are visible on the shelf supported by iron bars, which in turn are used for hanging pans and sieves. Everything tells us this is a place where the daily toil inspires and even revitalizes.

Natural things hold their own against sophisticated or superfluous elements which end looking as if they have been stripped of meaning. Wood, whatever its tone, provides warmth and serenity to a kitchen interior. Today the exact shade for everyone's personal taste can be found.

A little is a lot

This photo shows that with just a few elements are sufficient to clearly mark off the work areas in this kitchen

By the sink area there are two low cupboards, one space for the dishwasher and another one for the two door fridge.

The high up spaces on the wall have been put to good use by installing a cupboard with foldable doors and wooden shelving. As the sink leaves hardly any room on which to work on the gleaming stainless steel worktop, a small aluminum topped island has been set up in the center of the room. Two sets of matching drawers are underneath. The cooking unit has been designed as a totally independent piece standing on its own stainless steel legs. On both sides of the Imperial oven there are some drawers.

The burners are electric and the Gutman smoke extractor is as wide as the worktop. The continuity is ensured by the practical and aesthetic steel splashback.

The storage space has been taken care of by the wooden larder cupboard with interior lighting and five levels. The doors open and fold back so as not to block up the circulation or overstress the hinges.

Tips

A large built-in larder is test of the organizational ability of the home owner. Metal shelves and interior lighting have to go together with placing the seldom used products at the back.

Neatness and clear ideas

In this country style kitchen an equilibrium has been sought between the desire to create a feeling and the need to have all utensils at hand for efficient and imaginative cooking.

The radiant wood covering all the cupboards, the walls and the smoke extractor all give a sensation of durability and undeniable quality which together with the natural light coming in through the large windows from the garden allows the work to be done comfortably. As the ceiling is so high a metal bar with hooks has been hung near the window for saucepans and bouquets of dried flowers and aromatic herbs.

The room evokes country kitchens of bygone years but does not forgo the up to the minute design and organizational advances which enhance today's spaces.

The glass ceramic hob brings this traditional kitchen up to date. The control panel is located on one side and thus permits the cupboards and drawers on the front to maintain their uniform appearance.

The electrical appliances vital for family cooking are hidden out of sight. The dishwasher is camouflaged inside a cupboard under the sink and the oven is in a column unit.

Tips

The most frequently needed utensils *should be ready at hand but it is common sense not to put them on display if they are battered by so much use. Sometimes the best looking gadgets are also the most efficient and natural looking because modern designers enjoy recreating past models.*

Ovens

There are two types of ovens: built-in and freestanding ones. The former can form part of the cooking unit beneath the hob or they can be located in an independent block and at eye level. This is the best solution if the oven is used frequently and when you have enough space.

The ovens that form part of a traditional kitchen can be gas or electric. Below them it is common for there to be a tray for keeping pans and roasting trays. The doors always open downwards and can be left open to allow the food to cool. In the recent past the self-cleaning models have come into fashion, freeing the cook from having to scrap the grease off or having to use toxic products.

The microwave oven is now a fixed piece in the majority of kit-

chens, both for families or for one person households. It is quick, easy to use and goes down especially well among busy people or the just too lazy to cook. It can also serve as a complement for other cooking systems.

The noble room in the house

Here it is clear that the owners of this kitchen want to break down the barriers which define areas according to the social uses given to them.

In a typical family country house the kitchen is normally an area in which the staff work, or, alternatively, an area in which to exhibit traditional artisanal skills and flavors, with an equal emphasis on practicality and respect for the traditional forms. However, all this is always within a context of austerity aimed at reflecting and showing appreciation for the efforts of bygone generations.

Here the designers have decidedly gone for luxury, made evident by the materials and ornaments used in the detailing and trimmings and also manifested by all the appliances available for when the kitchen is working flat out.

In the wide recess, finished in white brick, the cooking zone has been fitted with a smoke extractor above it and a golden bar running across it from which to hang pans, pots and herbs to give an image of wise and prosperous activity.

In reality, today when time is the most precious asset, it is logical that the cookers should be geared towards saving time. It is also healthy, and reassuring, to know that traditions and gastronomic culture remains intact and that new tech is not only aimed at saving time but also at maintaining our daily habits.

The washing and preparation zone has a more restrained image but is equally elegant. Noble materials have been selected. The cupboards and drawers are faced in wood (the interiors too) and the worktop is of black granite. The double bowl sink area is of porcelain. The faucets are in stainless steel.

The decoration is finished off by the trimmed cornices, the light columns and the crystal showcases with blue rhomboids displaying the refined family china, perhaps handed down from mother to daughter with the recipes which attract the rest of the family to the appetizing table.

The dining room table top is of rounded edged crystal. It is supported by two sturdy fluted columns and the base is a grayish blue matching the rest of the furniture. The light brown reupholstered chairs, with rhomboidal backrests, indicates that the all-important kitchen is an area where the people must feel at ease, relaxing and socializing as they enjoy the food.

Sometimes it is a good idea to knock down a partition and to extend the kitchen into a dining area suitable for all occasions.

As the wall is slanted, it was decided to create upper cupboards of varying heights, which at the same time alleviate the visual heaviness of the toffee colored fronts.

The touch of light green on the lower faces adds a nuance of cheerful modernity to a kitchen dominated by the functionality.

There are other upbeat practical details: the glass cabinet by the wall with its internally lit shelves for storing utensils, other small objects or herbs and spices. The eye level built-in oven in an independent block liberates the space below the hob for storing big saucepans and dishes.

The preparation island, too, plays off solidness against lightness. A cupboard wide enough to contain the crockery and opening on both sides is situated underneath.

The other table end, supported by one aluminum leg serves as a dining table (nothing gets in the way of your legs) and a preparation worktop.

The all-purpose accessory cabinet on wheels with two large capacity drawers has a wood top and can hold or transport heavy pots or hot plates from the burners to the dining room next door.

Tips

*This is a close up of **the cupboard - height and length** to be decided- fitted halfway up the wall under the worktop. It is designed for storing taller objects which do not fit on the smaller shelves.*

On the far right the four power sockets as practical as they are aesthetic.

This urban style design draws together independent units from diverse sources to create a family kitchen covering all the necessities. The cooking zone consists of the oven, hob and smoke extractor.

It is perfectly balanced by the low cupboards on either side and above there are three levels of shelving. The transparent shiny blue plastic boxes eye catchingly allow the light to insinuate the contents.

A fresh idea for getting the most out of the kitchen space is the rectangular board that swivels around the pole holding it in place.

Perforations allow metal strips to be fixed for hanging heavy or bulky recipients on one side. Round the back there are steel bars and hooks for frequently used utensils (pans, pots and sieves) and, in the middle, rests the lectern for the enthusiasts of the art of cooking. It fits neatly into the corner and combines well with closed cupboards.

Tips

The wood units *divided into rectangles for storing books or the sound system give sobriety to the kitchen, which here forms part of the living area. The plastic drawers are apt for storing any kind of object although their location makes them more suitable for hiding away items not involved in the cooking process.*

Looking for one's own style

In this kitchen versatility and individualism are harmoniously combined. The glossy white fronts share the spotlight with the beige sides and bases of the low cupboards.

A contrast is offered by the upper cupboards and shelving for the crockery, widened in a gracious curve in the lower half and imitating in a minimalist way traditional sideboards. The green tone and transparent grips bestow a calmness on the zone.

This design aims at comfort through ergonomics. The oven and the sink are built-in to avoid having to bend and three different work heights have been established depending on the activity being carried out.

It is noteworthy the way the space left available by the cupboards is used to the full and the effective solutions for corners that could have been inefficiently exploited. Screwed to the wall there is a simple wooden board with bars at diverse heights for holding utensils (graters, scissors, etc.) which could get mislaid in drawers.

Of course there is the kitchen roll and hanging little pots here sets free space for other recipients in the larger drawers.

Tips

*Top scoring for ingenious design must go to the **sturdy circular wood** worktop which can be fitted into a corner. The circular sliding door conceals two metal rimmed rotating shelves for kitchen utensils. Its location next to the washing zone, and the way it sticks out, make it ideal as a preparation table.*

The good cooking store

In this kitchen the atmosphere is dictated by the sensation of specialization and order, like in an old ironmonger's or notions stores.

The sheer number of drawers with steel colored shell shaped grips seems to be proclaiming the capacity to store, or even file, everything in the kitchen.

Just like in the nineteenth century stores, the stainless steel ladder, movable along all the run of shelves, makes all the products in the cubbyholes or open cupboards reachable. Above the sink there are two glass shelves which match it in length.

The cooking zone, composed of a worktop and a smoke extractor, has been kept separate against another wall.

In the middle a marble topped island doubles as a preparation zone or a dining table, one end of which is over three groups of drawers. The back of these drawers is Carrera marble and separates off the leg room under the table. A crystal shelf suspended from the ceiling by two slender metal bars runs into the wall.

The color combination gives a cheerful, snug sensation, typical of very lived in family kitchens.

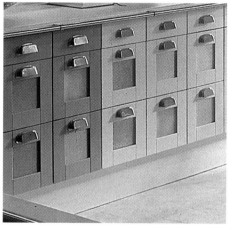

Tips

*When there are many **drawers with similar capacities** it is recommendable to organize where we place every utensil and object: put it near where it is used. It is common sense to store seldom used or heavy gadgets at the bottom. The upper cupboards are for tablecloths, cutlery and flat utensils.*

A homage to the good life

This kitchen, bathed in natural light coming in from the garden aims at reproducing the traditional kitchen spirit with white pine furniture but without falling into overindulgent nostalgia. Restrained class has been preferred to the country style manifest in the pilasters, the corner cornices and the separations between the units.

The kitchen has various functions. Obviously it is for food preparation, for storage and for eating in a social, leisurely way. Each function has its own space which does not intrude on the other. The room is warm, relaxed but not chaotic.

The central island with glass fronted cupboards in the middle and shelves at the two ends separates the work zone from the dining area. The sink, rinse bowl and draining board are countersunk into the amber wood worktop. On the wall two upper cupboards are either side of a high tech smoke extractor camouflaged behind an old chimney. The dining room is faithful to the same style with a long, unvarnished pine table in front of a cupboard into which the oven has been built.

The imaginative showcase for the crockery and the well stocked wine rack complete the declaration of allegiance to the good life.

Tips

Metal door grips *are simple but effective, a good solution for cupboard fronts that look too classic. Metal breaks the monotony of wood and adds luminosity.*

The high number of small apartments nowadays has pushed the interior designers into coming up with original, versatile solutions to get round the lack of space. Creativity and inspiration

are greatly valued if they result in furniture, albeit factory produced, which manages to meet the needs of good cooking and, even better, is alluring.

Often the vividness of the color provides some visual relief. Bold surfaces and textures tied in with combinations of materials, industrial or natural as necessary, have pushed aside established practices.

Clarity, neatness and comfort are the principal premises of contemporary style, a declaration of confidence and inhibition, staking

it all on such a forcefully inventive design that it outdoes the classic.

Contemporary style design is ideal for people without prejudices, used to mixing work with fun. Among these type of people it is common to find kitchens which open up onto the lounge or studio, fading out the distinction between public and private.

To avoid any one piece of furniture dominating over the others make sure they are conceptually cohesive. Go for restrained finishes and all-purpose materials and create a visual separation between the zones using wall paints, the lighting, or distinct flooring.

Originality as a synonym of elegance

The originality of this kitchen has been achieved without sacrificing any of its classic elegance. The clear separation of activities is based around the L shaped layout of the veneered high and

low cupboards in cream tones. The upper sections of the former are used like show cases. Storage is on the left and the washing zone on the right.

Both sections have synthetic worktops usable as preparation zones. Notice that below the sink zone there are cupboards, one of which contains the dishwasher. Below the work zone counter there

are drawers, the deepest ones at the bottom.

The corner makes you look again: it is attractive thanks to the luminous cupboard that displays its contents on swivel trays. The laminated aluminum fridge is on the near left, rounding off the visually striking design. The curved lines continue into the cooking zone which has been created around a

circular granite slab with a glass ceramic hob countersunk into it and resting over a white fronted curvaceous wood unit. On one side there is a small bar that runs into the half partition wall coming down like a slide chute. The final detail is the smoke extractor hanging from the ceiling like a lamp.

A not too frequent option

The dark tones give elegance and sobriety to this kitchen with diamond blue lacquered fronts and moldings. It opens onto the everyday dining zone in which the light shed by the grand windows contrasts with the formality of the design.

The cooking and storage zones have been located along the wall free of doors and windows. At both ends cupboards have been placed in the form of columns. They can be used as a pantry or to fit a fridge and independent freezer.

The glass ceramic hob is in the center while the two ovens are at eye level in the adjacent unit.

The telescopic smoke extractor is camouflaged inside the tiled chimney matching the wall behind the hob. The washing island is staggered upwards in three levels as it runs towards the wall. The serving area is the highest, the washing zone is in the middle and the preparation zone at the bottom. There is an overhanging ledge permitting one to work sitting down.

All of the worktops are granite, endorsed by its resistance, a quality also necessary for the sink with its soaking and washing bowls in stainless steel.

Tips

The trapezial shaped granite *topped dining table is supported by metal legs. It is wider on the side furthest from the wall to ensure the third diner has enough room. The cupboards on the central island open toward the cooking zone so as not to get in the way when serving meals on the other side.*

Clever design

When one is living in a tight space it is inevitable that the spaces are reduced to merely fulfilling their functions.

However, the host of practical and aesthetic solutions made available by modern kitchen design mean that one does not have to give up on the things which make a home more livable.

In this example the only free wall space is the triangle area and therefore the storage space had to be placed in the lower part in small modules with foldable doors.

The limited free spaces on the wall are covered by accessories, like the little pots for legumes on the shelves, or the metal bar supporting the bookshelves.

The white of the faces increases the luminosity, however, natural wood, and the warmth it offers, was preferred for the rest of the unit including the worktop, the cooking zone, the washing zone (with its two separate bowls of distinct depths) and the preparation zone.

The semicurve in the corners maximizes the workable area enabling small appliances, like the expresso cafeteria and the deep fryer, to fit in.

Tips

The little wall *on the center left of the photo is the base for a modest dining table, a simple formula for linking the two spaces without any mutual encroaching.*

The cloth backed chairs are a necessary dash of elegance and class.

Refined neatness

The apparently paradoxical union of two incompatible work zones, a kitchen and a piano, an instrument used regularly, show just how technical and aesthetically creative kitchen design has become.

Neither of these areas clashes with the other nor lacks elegance or functionality.

The kitchen has been divided into two fronts. The ovens are built into a dark wood paneled wall. The cupboard hand grips, using the same system applied to the cupboards along the right below the sink and work counter, are disguised as concave protruding metal edges.

The washing, preparation and cooking zone, with its gas hob, form a series of waist-high cupboards and drawers.

The white lacquered fronts offer an extremely neat, refined image that pushes to the back of the mind the echoes of the sixties of the original model.

The cupboards above the sink are divided into three sections two levels high. The lower level has a glass door and metal frame, brightening up the kitchen with its pleasant color.

Tips

The worktop lighting *has been solved by fixing a line of halogen spotlights inside a steel soffit with a plug at the end.*

In open kitchens this type of illumination complements the ambiental light coming from the studio or living room.

A washing peninsula

The aim in this kitchen was to give every work area sufficient space so that one can move around with total freedom. The cooking area is lower than the preparation zone to make it more comfortable for the cook.

The cooker and its ceramic hob are compact. The oven door is of steel and crystal. The generously sized drawers have steel handles. The only adornment necessary on

the smoke extractor above the hob is the purity of its lines.

The preparation zone has above it four cubbyhole type openings which are alternatively closed with glass doors or exposed.

On top of the wood worktop, a white Corian chopping board surface has been fitted. Its oval shape is mimicked by the bulky storage drawers.

Something even more original is the way the washing zone is on a peninsula coming out of the wall.

The lack of windows, in front of which the sink is traditionally placed, meant that another solution had to be found; here the sink is innovatingly perpendicular to the rest of the furniture. The dishwasher is built into the unit next to the washing area, easing the blending together of zones.

Tips

The ledge connected *to the ceiling by metal bars has an upper wood shelf and a lower one of glass. Due to its height and situation it has been assigned the function of providing specific lighting for the sink and of holding decorative or hardly used objects. The plants are one option which livens up the corner and do not get in the way.*

Classically impacting

This kitchen combines white cupboards, drawers varnished in a chestnut color and wood framed glass cases, some of them with handles and others with shell shaped grips, to give the room a warm feeling, an aim aided by the one-piece backed chairs and oval wood table.

The innovating, modern touch is provided by the kitchen equipment, two sophisticated built-in ovens in a separate block, a gas hob, griddle and a glass ceramic hotplate. Such cooking power calls for a forceful smoke extractor. This one is steel, as are the drawers for large pots situated below the burners.

The Combi fridge, fitted into a recess by the entrance to the kitchen, has a freezer in the upper part.

The medium height section of the wall has been tiled in green while the upper wall section, as well as the side of the column on the left separating the fridge from the ovens, has been painted indigo blue to match the upholstery of the chairs. This conspicuous detail gains in impact thanks to the halogen spotlights built into a wooden soffit and into the ceiling.

The floor is tiled with small white and blue squares.

Tips

The sink bowls, *including a little one for soaking, have been installed in a corner of the synthetic worktop, leaving more free space on either side. The cupboards underneath have sufficient space for the waste disposal and the standard cleaning products.*

Natural efficiency

Today's apartments have made it vital to have a space fitted out for eating, integrated into the kitchen or communicating with it through one of the work zones. This type of kitchen no longer implies lack of room but rather shows how lifestyles have changed cooking habits.

Here the aim was to create an efficient space overcoming the lack of natural light in the kitchen zone, especially important because the eating area is regularly used. The furniture had to be designed with natural materials which contribute to the sense of organization. To this end, nothing is better than modular units, high and low cupboards closed off with sturdy amber doors and a few glass cabinets. Under the upper cupboards there are fluorescent tubes. The light is intensified by the white wall tiles and on the worktop.

The oven is in the middle and the microwave to the left of the sink at eye level. There are also a dishwasher and a fridge.

Placing the hob in the worktop separating the dining area off is a clever move for it helps when serving meals and the position of the stainless steel smoke extractor does not take space away from the storage cupboards.

Tips

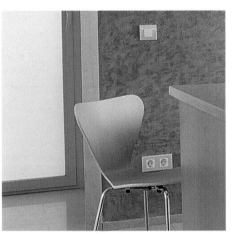

The walls free of furniture *have been painted in a strawberry color adding life to all the room and taking advantage of the natural light coming in. Also the varnished parquet flooring intensifies the light reflection.*

Compact furniture

The kitchen of this modern house is fitted out with compact furniture integrated into the open space which looks like the alcove in an old apartment.

As it is an out of town home, the owners only use the kitchen sporadically and for modest meals. Therefore it was not necessary to amplify the work space. A simple U shaped distribution sufficed for the everyday needs without having to fall back on sophisticated new inventions which would not have been fully taken advantage of anyway.

The white laminated floor and wall cupboards with their simple plastic handles perfectly satisfy the storage necessities.

The washing zone is next to the entrance, opposite the cooking zone. The camouflaged conventional smoke extractor is turned on by pulling the front forwards.

The contrast to the uniformity imposed by the white of the cupboards and walls comes from the little black shelves on the wall and the black board with the built-in spotlights hanging from the ceiling to add to the soft lighting of the worktops.

Tips

The gap where the staircase *emerges has determined the clearly minimalist kitchen design. The nearness of the eating zone reduces the bother of having to go back and forth.*

This photo demonstrates that it is never impossible to install a kitchen in any space if one believes in modern interior decoration and leaves aside superfluous, capricious details.

As only one wall was available, all the elements are in one run either above or below the worktop of natural tone varnished wood strips. At the far end is the sink bowl and in the middle the cooking hob. The oven is underneath. The reduced space available meant that a smaller than normal dishwasher and fridge were chosen, the fronts of which match the cupboards and drawers.

The furniture faces are veneered and varnished while amber, very warm and in fashion, was applied to the sides and the stainless steel smoke extractor zone.

The walls and ceiling were painted vanilla in keeping with the synthetic flooring. This gives a more spacious sensation. Halogen spotlights were built into the ceiling and underneath the cupboards for general and specific lighting respectively.

The two wood framed glass sliding doors open up to reveal the dining area and to allow in the natural light.

Tips

Cupboards as narrow *as this one oblige the cook to get rid of anything superfluous and impose tight organization. Modern manufacturers have put on the market models adaptable to these spaces, the most recommendable being those with one continuous run.*

A green corner

This kitchen is so big that a dining area for every day use can be situated in an adjacent zone near the clearly separated washing zone.

Apart from the doors and windows on the right the walls were free of architectural interruptions and fully taken advantage of to install high built-in cupboards with doors opening upwards just below the ceiling.

Along with a space for provisions and an eye level oven, there is a Combi refrigerator with a laminated maple colored wood front in keeping with the other furniture.

For the cooking zone a large cooker with burners and a grill was selected. The splashback behind the cooker was paneled in stainless steel to create a block with the smoke extractor and the drawers

for casserole dishes and other saucepans.

A sheet of white marble covers the worktops and the intermediate wall zone, the rest being painted in a sprightly green in tune with the blinds which provide shade for the window and the gallery.

The flooring is lighter than the furniture to tone down the impact of the green.

Tips

The general lighting *comes from spotlights built into the ceiling and the specific lighting is supplied by the smoke extractor and the middle part of the preparation zone. There are also spotlights in the ceiling of the dining area and a lamp focused on the table.*

Wood implies warmth and is easily swept but it lack the qualities of impermeability and resistance to humidity so is not recommended for heavily used floors.

Tiles are resistant, impermeable, cheap and come in almost every color under the rainbow. Their only drawback is their hardness and slipperiness.

Ceramic also creates a homely sensation and comes in many textures, colors, shapes and sizes. However its porosity means it tends to absorb spillages and its average price is a little expensive.

Slate is a material renowned for its resistance and impermeability. It is available in various colors and sizes, although big slabs are to be avoided because they break more easily. The finish is natural and rough so its surface is hard and cold to touch.

Limestone slabs are another possibility which comes in diverse colors, textures and patterns. They are very resistant to heat, water and cleaning materials, are hardwearing and need little maintenance. The disadvantages are that they are hard, cold and noisy. The seams are difficult to keep clean.

Cork tiles are one of the most recent presentations and have quickly found a niche in the market due to their low price and easy installation. A varnish finish must be applied to avoid humidity seeping through. It is very quiet but has the drawback of being on the dull side.

Vinyl is a plastic that comes in rolls or tiles. It is soft, quiet, impermeable, resistant but not slippery. It is easy to see that it is artificial so it should be chosen for its patterns, not when trying to imitate natural materials.

Linoleum is quite similar to vinyl although it is dearer because it is made of natural materials. It is quiet, warm, easy to maintain although it needs polish and it is worth watching the seams so that water does not seep through when it inevitably peels off the floor over time.

A high up cupboard

In a medium sized kitchen, like in the photo, installing cupboards above the rectangular window is a good idea to take advantage of the limited storage space available.

These cupboards were placed high up because there was no alternative. The wood edged glass doors open upwards; their

transparency creating a sensation of lightness.

The lower shelves of the cupboards, designed as a draining rack, have nothing underneath and are easily kept free of dust and grease.

Below the sink and hob the cupboards and drawers are standard. The front of the run of cup-boards are laminated, varnished wood in a warm chestnut color, including the dishwasher door to the right of the sink. The steel handles provide contrast and will last many years.

The modern kitchen has come to be associated with efficient organization of all the elements stored there, whether they be work utensils, food products or cleaning materials.

As these accessories are related to storage, they are normally located near a wall and can be divided into high units, intermediate units and low units. Cupboards or drawers, varying in width, can be fixed to the wall. They are less deep than their floor counterparts to avoid knocking your head. In general, low floor standing cupboards have a standard width but they may vary to fill a gap between blocks, a few even being as shallow as ten centimeters. There are flat drawers specially for holding cutlery or chopping boards. However, on the wall above worktops and below upper cupboards many varieties of storage can be found like small glass cabinets or narrow shelves for herbs, spices and little containers.

What has most advanced are the systems for buffers and extendible drawers in which big round or ovaled pans and dishes can fit. Also new interior casings for drawers designed for cutlery or small pots have appeared. Kitchen corners are no longer written off zones thanks to the swivel trays and boards that open outwards on ingenious brackets. Awkward spaces can be filled with freestanding towers with swivel ledges and shelves. Task lighting can also be fitted.

Neither does the imagination have limits in the question of materials for finishes. All are accepted, wood, crystal, metal and synthetics. Vivid colors are no longer tabu, nor is it imperative that the shapes are regular. It is now more common for there to be curvaceous fronts to the units, not as a caprice of the designer but as an audacious response to a space problem.

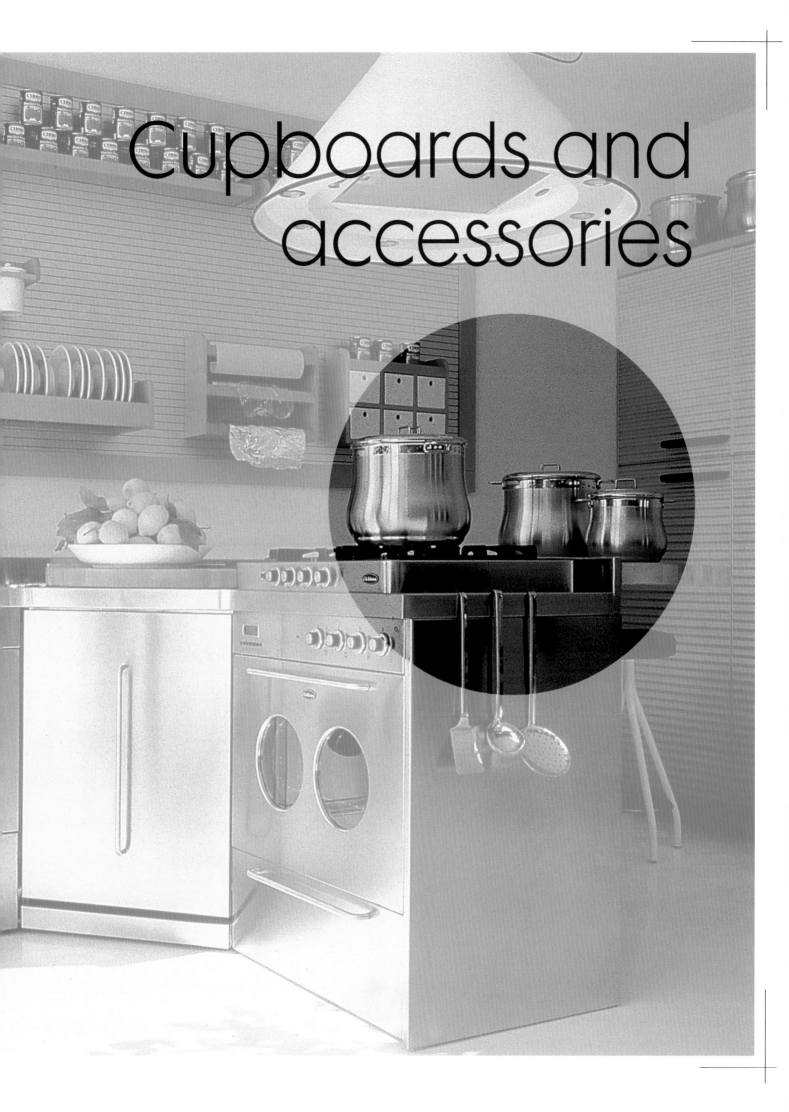

Cupboards and accessories

Cupboards

A vivid pistachio color

The originality of these two independent modular units stems from the combination of two materials and colors apparently quite incompatible. The pistachio green colored cupboards are partially fitted into two boards stuck to a wooden plinth. The protruding part of the cupboards only needs the support of one metal leg in the middle making cleaning underneath easier. The module on the left has been used to fit the oven and the microwave into. The upper part is a cupboard and the lower part high capacity drawers. The right part of the central zone is an ideal place for storing foods and other goods which have not found a home in other parts of the module.

A daring crystal frame

The tendency for the kitchen to be not just a work place but also somewhere for spending time together has pushed the designers into presenting new cupboard models which break away from the opaque fronted modular style of the last decades. This built in cupboard includes five adjustable shelves envisaged for keeping the everyday crockery and glassware. The aesthetic attractiveness of the unit stems from the two forty five centimeter wide metal profiled crystal doors, a pragmatic style now in fashion, playing with what you se and what you don't.

A place for everything and everything in its place

This practical module, thirty centimeters wide, incorporates a clothes basket on guided runners which can be pulled out to the maximum offering practicality, lightness, and accessibility yet without sacrificing aesthetics.

Everything fits in this corner

This cupboard is especially designed for short of space kitchens. Although from outside the model appears to be the standard rectangular shape, inside there is shelving adapted for circular containers, offering greater accessibility and fitting more in. The functionality of this piece originates in it being able to go snugly into a corner in a kitchen where every inch counts.

A food pantry

The first purpose of this pantry cupboard with its difficult to beat storage capacity is to keep in order the stocks, here tending towards the reserves rather than every day usage. The side has little height adjustable ledges, imitating a refrigerator, while the back has sliding trays which come forward when the door is opened. The blue curved front with a wide handle half way up is the unique decorative element on this modular piece. White and blue combine with the gleaming steel worktops.

Clean waste.

Ecological awareness means that today society rightly insists that household waste is sorted and recycled. This is reflected in the design of this sixty centimeter wide unit, the base of which has been fully taken advantage of by installing three substantial garbage containers below the bowl.

Down below and at hand.

What is most striking about this cupboard is not the pleasing appearance of the steel front and matching worktop, but rather the depth: seventy five centimeters, distributed into two drawers and adding up to one third more storage space than what is normally needed for the cooking pots, the size and weight of which are tell tale signs that cooking is taken seriously in this home. Another plus is the runners that permit the drawer to be totally pulled out and rubber blocks which silence the whole opening and closing process

Remember

• The typical dresser that stood in our grandparents' kitchen with its wide central shelf is still a good example of efficient distribution for a larder.

• Even if some space is left empty it is worth separating the products stored in the larder and those that go in the fridge.

• The larder or pantry must be away from the main work area.

• When buying a fridge-freezer consider not only its capacity but also its energy consumption, noise level, speed of de-frosting and its emission of gases.

Drawers

At room temperature

These wicker baskets are for storing fresh produce that does not need refrigeration, like bread or greens. Inserted in a wooden frame, they are dismountable for the easy removal of crumbs and shells. A useful idea and neat to look at.

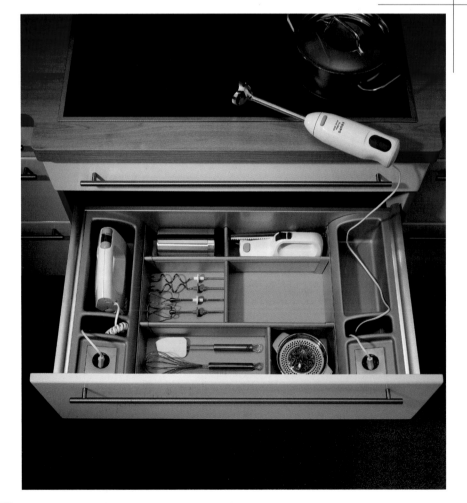

Energy incorporated

These drawers are the antithesis of a tailor's drawer, usually brimming with odds and ends. These drawers are just the opposite: they come in a wide range of interior modules with adaptable linings so that different sized objects can be stored away but easily found when needed. ìA place for everything and everything in its placeî was never truer. Domestic appliances, utensils and gadgets can be seen at a glance and used by plugging them into the built in power sockets. You do not have to worry about the lead not reaching.

Together but not mixed

This wood liner can be fitted into any drawer to prevent knives or other sharp objects from getting damaged, as may happen in plastic drawers. It is long-lasting, tasteful and traditional.

Four in one

Camouflaged behind a door that opens like a drawer there are three pull-out shelves used for storing long life food products and bottles; very practical for the forgetful.

Double height

Beneath the wood worktop there is a double-tray drawer sixty centimeters wide. The top tray slides back to allow access to the second level without removing the first. It is a comely way of keeping the daily cutlery neat.

Silver spoons

This drawer makes manifestly clear the thorough and thoughtful attention to detail that is paid to get the most out of kitchen units. The space has been distributed on three levels with a holding capacity for one hundred and forty pieces of cutlery. The container is crafted out of beechwood and lined in felt to avoid the silver rusting. For the everyday cutlery a multi-layered wood tray can be used.

Neat drawers

These units were chosen thinking how to make the housewife as comfortable as possible, so that they feel good in an ordered space. The drawers of different sizes and heights neatly store all types of recipients, and the metal dividers provide stability and avoid scratching when taking anything out. This kitchen has a traditional, homely feel to it. The gray limestone worktop and classically simple handles epitomize good taste while the space distribution and detailing (edges, automatic closure, etc.) make it evident that the design is totally modern.

Cakes and spices

This is the tops if you are looking for order and functionality when tidying away accessories and odds and ends in the drawers beneath the worktops. As well as hiding utensils time-honored practice assigned to hanging on the wall (whisks, sieves, etc), specific provision has been made for tin-foil rollers, herb jars, sharp knives and the rolling pin.

A stylish curve

Heavy not too frequently used pots should be kept out of sight but accessible. Drawers below worktops form a natural part of today's kitchen.

In the right place

On both sides of the draining boards there are cupboards in which to place the cleaning utensils and the recyclable waste bucket. The dishwasher is neatly tucked away in a corner.

Furniture

Preserve reserve

One of the latest inventions for storage is the creation of larder cupboards inside which extendible shelves and drawers are combined. In addition to their versatility (they can store preserves, pots, packets, boxes and jars) the visual monotony of shelves of the same height can be broken. As they are pull-out everything is handy and visible at a glance. The handle of the drawers is a hollow and the trays are stylishly metal rimmed.

Clean and secure

The space below the sink has always traditionally been reserved for waste disposal and the storage of the cleaning materials. In this model the cylindrical garbage container is hinged on the door leaving the other space free for the closable metal container which keeps the cleaning materials safely out of the way. Another plus is the aluminum base resistant to any drips or spillages.

Sliding storage

In contemporary design kitchens the space is arranged so as to keep out of sight all utensils which contribute nothing to the aesthetics, things like casserole dishes, pans and other cooking recipients. Wide drawer models like these solve the problem keeping the pans hidden but at hand in the bulky base. These drawers have no tendency to topple when fully opened thanks to the guiding, balancing rods supported by four wheels.

No head blows

This cupboard with an upwardly opening door is designed to be installed high up. Here it has been fixed with a glass front, but others are possible. It looks better with wide units.

Salt and pepper

This piece takes advantage of the space with intelligent internal distribution and the mechanism by which, when the door is opened, the metal basket slide outwards making all the contents instantly reachable.

Just pull

This model is reminiscent of the traditional pharmacy cabinets with their extractable racks and double sided openings. The trays can be placed at different heights for the convenience of the user.

The ideal depth for storage *shelves is less than sixty centimeters. Beyond this, putting one's arm in can be tricky. Do not leave toxic materials or sharp objects within the reach of children.*

Wood and steel

As the space traditionally occupied by the oven has been left vacant, two maple units with stainless steel pull out trays have been installed. They are for storing assorted unsightly kitchen utensils in an easy to get at place.

A smart idea

A smart idea for when you do not want to fit the fridge into the wall or wedge it between cupboards is to decorate it with shelving on the sides, gray brackets hiding away the screws. They serve as a larder and a handy ledge making the room look lived in while helping to keep everything in its place.

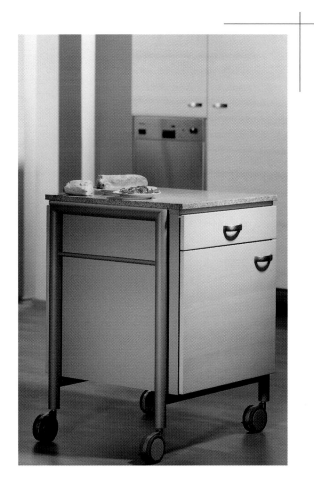

Service on wheels

This small model is composed of a cupboard and a drawer with a granite worktop. It is an extremely comfortable aid due to the wheels. Combining distinct materials (wood, metal and granite) is a typical solution in today's interior design which places emphasis on flexibility and functionality rather than on the aesthetic appearance. However, the latter is not scorned. The versatility of this model makes it suitable for occupying a gap in a studio, an apartment, a compact family home or in the work kitchen of a small company. It always adapts to the needs of the diverse users.

Sinks

In soak

This is an innovational curved sink unit for a small, not heavily used kitchen. The draining zone has been set up behind the faucets. One side area is thus free for the cleaning utensils and the other is for soaking.

Misleadingly simple

This small one bowl sink combines its traditional, simple form and distribution with a modern synthetic resistant material. The gap for brushes and clothes is a resourceful idea.

A white sink.

This sink reminds us of the days when a house wife had nothing else to help her other than the force of her hands. However, the white surface is misleading for there is nothing at all traditional about it, except its functionality. The work space has been divided into three for cutting, soaking and washing the ingredients to be cooked. The little space for soaking the greens ranks high for its practicality, placed in such a way that water arrives effortlessly from the faucet. The grooved surface is slightly sloped so that the draining board runs down to the sink.

Stainless steel

The stainless steel version has been designed curved in case it were necessary to fit it into a work corner. The novelty lies in the plentiful drainage outlets, on the draining board, in the sink and in the supplementary hole.

Remember

• *One of the most in fashion options is the sliding cupboard with three different containers for recyclable and organic waste. There are models available which adapt to the space of each individual kitchen or with a direct chute from the worktop to the garbage disposal.*

Unusual placement

This original placing for a sink, not against a window as is standard but rather in the middle of the room, seems to imply that preparing the food is so interesting no views are necessary. The large worktop and thick legs give a sensation of resistance.

The ideal height for a sink *is five centimeters below the flexed elbow. Try too avoid using sinks with deep bowls; over time forced or unnatural positions will produce back ache and bad posture.*

Remember

• *Sinks are normally located near a window to make working at them more pleasant. The rim should be five centimeters below the flexed elbow.*

• *It is recommendable crockery and cutlery are stored nearby.*

• *Two bowls allow the work to be divided. One bowl can be for washing and the other for filling pots or rinsing. Make sure they are deep enough for cleaning large pots.*

• *In big kitchens if the worktop is a long way from the sink, a small auxiliary bowl comes in handy.*

Not demanding

In this relaxed decoration kitchen a stainless steel sink with two sizable bowls has been installed. The long mixer faucet can be directed at the bowl you are working at.

The washing corner

This old very deep bowl, tucked away in a corner, continues to fulfil its function but most of the washing is done by the dishwasher.

Smoke extractors and cookers

A telescopic cooking hood

The telescopic hoods and the conventional ones do not normally have the thick tube associated with the decorative ones. Instead they are camouflaged inside runs of cupboards or imitate old chimneys.

A classic structure

The cooking worktop, the oven and the smoke extractor form a very practical compact block in conventionally sized kitchens. An aluminum splashback has been placed in all the cooking zone to avoid splatters . Pleasant specific lighting is supplied by the halogen lights built into the smoke extractor.

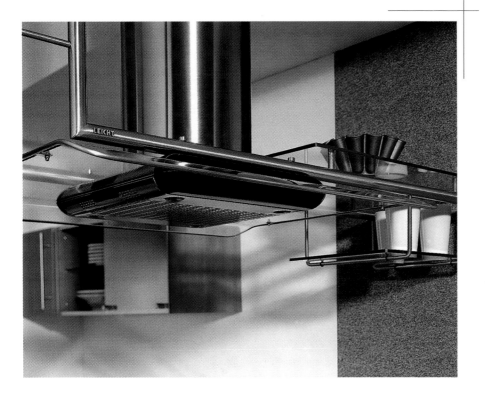

Practical and decorative

This is an original and interesting smoke extractor consisting of a tube and an octagonal shaped sheet of glass. Apart from being useful as a shelf for oils and pots always in use, this smoke extractor is innovative in that it uses electronic technology to get rid of the fumes: a great idea becoming consolidated in the world of kitchen design.

The ideal height for the cooker *is ten to fifteen centimeters below the bent elbow. Annoying splashes on the worktops can be avoided if the kitchen design places them slightly above the burners.*

A wide cooker

The burners can be laid out in a line of four instead of two by two. This will leave some space behind them for storing ingredients, oils and herbs.

Lighting

Lighting without shadows

Spotlights embedded in the ceiling are becoming more common for they avoid bothersome shadows. One can choose between halogen lights or low consumption light bulbs. It is convenient to have more than one switch so that you do not have to turn all the lights on at the same time.

General lighting

These little lamps hanging from the ceiling offer general and specific lighting simultaneously. As there are no cupboards on the walls a light bulb which emits non-glaring light has been chosen so that the shadows are not annoying.

Intimacy

Using candles as an alternative source of lighting gives warmth and intimacy difficult to get with other sources.

Original solutions

This is an example of improvised specific lighting to light a kitchen without a smoke extractor.

This is a spotlight supported on a wall bracket to illuminate a preparation zone.

• *When a room is small and there is no possibility of opening it up into the next room, space can be gained by using sliding doors or introducing windows between the rooms so that light can enter.*

• *Noisy or boring housework (washing and ironing) which are not daily activities related to cooking should be done outside the kitchen. Or if this is not possible, set up a space away from the cooker.*

• *Some colors are more common in kitchens than others because they have connotations of cleanliness and being professional (whites and creams).*

• *Other colors like gray make bright colors the focal point and neutralize strong lighting. Blues give a summery feeling and are especially appropriate if there is a lack of natural light. Yellow and cream tones go well with natural materials. Summing up, colors are worth studying to get the most out of the decoration.*

• *A good way of breaking the monotony of non-personalized furniture is combining colors and materials. However, if we are not in a position to change the colors we can introduce new accessories which add color and different shapes.*

Acknowledgements

NOLTE: 10, 12, 36, 54, 60, 76, 78, 88, 112, 120, 121, 119, 124/**SIEMATIC:** 14, 16, 18, 72 , 80, 90, 108, 109, 113, 114 115, 116, 117, 118, 119/**ALSA/LEICHT:** 62, 66, 72, 92, 120, 115, 116, 125/**TIELSA:** 20, 42 44, 82/**MIELE:** 8, 28, 38, 74, 86/**GRUCCO:** 68, 84, /**RATIONAL:** 26/**ALLMILLMO:** 40, 46, 48, 56, 58, 108, 119/**SCHIFFINI CINQUETERRE:** 22/**EUGENI PONS:** 24, 25, 29, 30, 31, 32, 33, 34, 35, 38, 74, 95, 97, 99, 101, 103.